TO: THE WORLD'S GREATEST DADDY

♡ WITH LOVE ♡

FROM: _____

MY DADDY

MY DADDY'S NAME IS: _____.

HE IS _____ **YEARS OLD.**

HIS JOB IS: _____.

HIS FAVORITE COLOR IS: _____.

HIS FAVORITE FOOD IS: _____.

MY DADDY

HIS HAIR COLOR IS: _____.

HIS EYE COLOR IS: _____.

HIS FAVORITE THING TO DO IS: _____

_____.

HE ALWAYS SAYS: _____.

MY DADDY

HE IS GOOD AT COOKING: _____.

HE LIKES TO WEAR: _____.

HIS FAVORITE THING TO WATCH ON TV IS:

_____.

HE LIKES TO GO: _____.

THIS IS A PICTURE OF ME AND MY DADDY:

YOU ARE A
SUPERHERO
JUST LIKE

_____•

I LOVE WHEN YOU CALL ME

_____ •

YOU MAKE ME LAUGH WHEN YOU

_____ •

I LOVE
WHEN YOU

_____ •

MY FAVORITE THING
TO DO WITH YOU IS

_____ .

THIS IS A PICTURE OF ME AND
MY DADDY HAVING FUN:

YOU ARE SO
GOOD AT

_____●

I LOVE YOU BECAUSE

_____•

I WANT TO GO

_____

WITH YOU.

I KNOW YOU LOVE ME BECAUSE

_____ •

YOU ARE SPECIAL BECAUSE

_____●

THIS IS A PICTURE OF A PARTY FOR MY DADDY:

WHEN YOU HUG
ME I FEEL

_____ •

I LOVE TO PLAY

_____

WITH YOU.

YOU TAUGHT ME
HOW TO

_____ •

YOU ARE SO MUCH FUN WHEN YOU

_____ •

I THINK IT'S SILLY WHEN YOU

_____ •

THIS IS A PICTURE OF THE AWARD YOU DESERVE:

I WANT TO GIVE YOU

_____

AS A PRESENT.

I WANT YOU TO
TEACH ME

_____ •

YOU ARE SO

_____●

THE BEST THING WE EVER DID TOGETHER IS

_____●

THIS IS A PICTURE OF MY DADDY:

WHEN I GET OLDER I WANT TO

_____

WITH YOU.